D0810584

Praise for *The Old Fashioned*

"The making of mixed drinks, especially among bourbon aficionados, is steeped in ritualistic purity and exacting particularity of preparation, and this is especially true of the Old Fashioned. This book is for those who love the drink and bourbon in all its many incarnations, including those who take pride in Kentucky and associations with its signal beverage."

—Richard Taylor, former poet laureate of Kentucky

"The Martini has several books recounting its history and extolling its virtues, so it is about time that the Old Fashioned, which also has a signature glass, had a book devoted to its history and recipes."

—Susan Reigler, coauthor of
The Kentucky Bourbon Cocktail Book

"Albert W. A. Schmid has done an excellent job researching this cocktail and produced a very enjoyable book. I look forward to adding it to my library."

—Michael R. Veach, author of
Kentucky Bourbon Whiskey: An American Heritage

The Old Fashioned

The
Old Fashioned

*An Essential Guide to the
Original Whiskey Cocktail*

Albert W. A. Schmid
Foreword by John Peter Laloganes

UNIVERSITY PRESS OF KENTUCKY

Scholarly publisher for the Commonwealth, serving Bellarmine
University, Berea College, Centre College of Kentucky, Eastern Kentucky
University, The Filson Historical Society, Georgetown College, Kentucky
Historical Society, Kentucky State University, Morehead State University,
Murray State University, Northern Kentucky University, Transylvania
University, University of Kentucky, University of Louisville, and Western
Kentucky University.
All rights reserved.

Editorial and Sales Offices: The University Press of Kentucky
663 South Limestone Street, Lexington, Kentucky 40508-4008
www.kentuckypress.com

17 16 15 14 13   5 4 3 2 1

Library of Congress Cataloging-in-Publication Data

Schmid, Albert W. A.
  The old fashioned : an essential guide to the original whiskey cocktail /
Albert W. A. Schmid.
      pages cm
  Includes bibliographical references and index.
  ISBN 978-0-8131-4173-2 (hardcover : alk. paper) — ISBN 978-0-8131-4174-9
(epub) (print) — ISBN 978-0-8131-4175-6 (pdf) (print) 1. Cocktails.
2. Whiskey. I. Title.
  TX951.S4157 2013
  641.87′4—dc23

                            2012042475

 This book is printed on acid-free paper meeting
the requirements of the American National Standard
for Permanence in Paper for Printed Library Materials.

Manufactured in the United States of America.

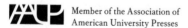 Member of the Association of
American University Presses

To my wife, Kimberly Schmid.
We have an old-fashioned love.

Thank you for your love and support,
and for saving me.

Contents

Foreword

In the current era, there is profound interest in and excitement about the cocktail. The bartender and mixologist are elevating alchemy to new levels of prestige by applying ingenuity and passion to their craft. Professionals and enthusiasts alike are invigorating the beverage industry with a renewed emphasis on the classics, representing a more simple time. The average American is consuming better-quality drinks nowadays, and in locations that are more accessible than ever before.

The Old Fashioned: An Essential Guide to the Original Whiskey Cocktail is a must-read book for all those who find pleasure as an epicurean. Albert W. A. Schmid's concise yet seminal work unravels the complex tale of the evolution of one of America's most significant drinks—the Old Fashioned. This book educates us in the nuances of drinking in style and fashion—tied to history and a timeless sense of place.

Through anecdotal storytelling and insightful prose, the origins of the Old Fashioned Whiskey Cocktail are revealed—weaving in the significant contributors who have added depth and complexity to this concoction over the years. Albert makes it a pleasure to revisit the past, and his pragmatic approach to the narrative yields an exciting, well-researched story that resonates emotionally with the reader. With intelligent humor and wit, his inquiry provides great insight and delivers high-quality entertainment.

The state of Kentucky is the birthplace of this celebrated and enduring cocktail. For me, three things come to mind when I think of Kentucky—bourbon (the foundation of the Old Fashioned), the Old Fashioned Whiskey Cocktail (originating at Louisville's Pendennis Club), and Albert Schmid (a true gentleman and a scholar). Albert is charismatic and charming, as well as modest and sincere. Upon meeting him for the first time, our conversation flowed freely, as if we were longtime friends from some previous era. In addition to being an accomplished sommelier and chef, Albert has become one of the most influential educators and speakers in the beverage industry and has won numerous awards and accolades for his work.

But he is also a relentlessly curious intellectual who is equally comfortable discussing spirits and cocktails as he is beer and wine. Schmid's passion for the Old Fashioned Whiskey Cocktail is apparent in these pages, as is his desire to communicate the alluring qualities of this classic drink.

As a sommelier, author, educator, and overall epicurean, I have come to appreciate "times gone by" and certain elements of the "good life" that I am blessed with. I must admit, during my review of the manuscript, I was enticed and inspired to retrieve the necessary ingredients from my spirits cabinet and replicate an Old Fashioned Whiskey Cocktail from one of the many recipes found within this book. Schmid teaches us how to suitably indulge with authenticity and sincerity. The Old Fashioned is triumphant—all hail this book! You will be more than delighted.

—*John Peter Laloganes*
  The Wine and Beverage Academy of Chicago
  2012 International Association of Culinary
  Professionals Award of Excellence—
  Sommelier of the Year

Preface

In 2011 Warner Brothers released a romantic comedy called *Crazy, Stupid, Love* starring Steve Carell, Julianne Moore, Ryan Gosling, Emma Stone, Marisa Tomei, and Kevin Bacon, among others. The plot is bittersweet, with a strong message: don't ignore love. As the story unfolds, the audience is introduced to Ryan Gosling's character, Jacob, who is a handsome paramour. Jacob is very successful in luring women home for, shall we say, romantic purposes. Part of Jacob's method, once he has a woman at his home, is to prepare her a cocktail as he listens to her talk about whatever is on her mind. We watch as Jacob makes the cocktail: he drops a sugar cube into a thick-bottomed glass, adds Angostura bitters, elegantly mixes the two together with a metal muddler, adds whiskey, and peels a large slice of orange zest, which he twists over the glass before placing it in the drink. The drink Jacob hands to his inamorata is clearly an Old Fashioned Whiskey Cocktail. Later, the use of bourbon is confirmed by the presence of a bottle of Pappy Van Winkle on the nightstand as the couple cuddles in bed. The cocktail acts as an allegory for the movie's plot.

Of all the cocktails for Jacob to use in the art of seduction, the Old Fashioned is the most poetic drink he could choose. The bittersweet whiskey-flavored beverage is simple to make but requires practice to perfect. The process of muddling the fruit (as some recipes call for) can be very seductive, if done in the right way by the right person. The ingredients are basic ones that mix very well, the aroma is sweet, and the flavor draws the drinker in and leaves her wanting more—not to mention the effects of alcohol, which are known to help people shed their inhibitions. The Old Fashioned is the perfect drink of seduction.

I did not always feel this way about the Old Fashioned. The first time I consumed one, I was not impressed. As I think back, it is clear to me that the person who made that drink did not understand how to make an Old Fashioned, did not show the proper love and care in mixing the drink, and probably did not enjoy his job. The bartender was young, most likely tending bar at night to afford graduate school during the day. That was more than twenty-five years ago in a college-town bar. Today, there is a resurgence of the craft of making cocktails. People are taking up the vocation of bartending with the careful precision of someone planning a career in law or academia. This new group of bartenders cares not only for the customer but also for the product they serve. Both are treated with the respect and care they are due. The bartender facilitates a symbiotic relationship between the customer and the cocktail, each relying on the other for survival. There is no better time to enjoy the Old Fashioned Whiskey Cocktail. Cheers!

—*Albert W. A. Schmid*
Louisville, Kentucky

The Old Fashioned

I

The Old Fashioned Whiskey Cocktail

THE ORIGINAL COCKTAIL?

The Old Fashioned Whiskey Cocktail—the Old Fashioned, for short[1] (and sometimes referred to as the Stubby Collins)[2]—is a classic American cocktail.[3] Although some say it is an adaptation from another cocktail—perhaps the Whiskey Cobbler or the Whiskey Cocktail[4]—others argue that it is the original cocktail.[5] The Old Fashioned has been described as "a truly magnificent cocktail,"[6] "the only cocktail really to rival the martini,"[7] and "one of the immortals: strong, square-jawed, with just enough civilization to keep you from hollerin' like a mountain-jack."[8] That's not bad for a drink that most sources say originated in the Bluegrass State.[9]

The Old Fashioned also led to other adaptations, such as the Mint Julep. Some older recipes for the Old Fashioned called for a sprig of mint and were described as "Juleps made the Old Fashioned Way."[10] According to the authors of *The Official Harvard Student Agencies Bartending Course,* the only two ingredients distinguishing the Old Fashioned and the Mint Julep are the bitters in the Old Fashioned and the garnishes in the two drinks: orange slice, cherry, and lemon twist for the Old Fashioned, and sprig of mint for the Julep.[11] Traditionally, a cocktail always includes bitters, which separates it from a julep or a toddy. The cocktail has the added distinction of being the original morning drink,[12] like a glass of orange juice or a cup of coffee today. In contrast, a julep is a sweetened alcoholic beverage that usually features mint and is consumed at midday (meaning any time from breakfast to dinner), and a toddy is a sweetened alcoholic beverage that can be served hot at the end of the day.

Ted Haigh (aka Dr. Cocktail) observes that the Old Fashioned eventually evolved into an "ugly slurry that has nothing to do with the original drink,"[13] which Brad Thomas Parsons (author of *Bitters*) refers to as "the fruit salad" approach.[14] The modern drink is actually a return to the historical version: a simple mixture of a little sugar, a little water (or simple syrup in their place), bitters, whiskey, and a slice of orange or lemon peel—a recipe that delights palates all over the world. The early versions differ from what most people think of as an Old Fashioned in that they lack fruit. The limited number of ingredients, the simplicity of the recipe, and the need to make the low-quality whiskey of the past palatable suggest that the Old Fashioned predates other cocktails.

The Old Fashioned is now on the beverage menu of most bars that serve cocktails, and no cocktail book is complete without at least one recipe for the Old Fashioned. But at what point did this cocktail become "old-fashioned" as opposed to a new concoction, which it must have been at some point? As with most great things, there is myth and there is truth. Part of the lore is that the term *cocktail* dates to 1776 in Elmsford, New York, where the owner of a bar ran out of wooden stirrers and substituted cocks' tail feathers. During that time, cocktails were also known as "roosters." In 1806, in response to a reader's question, a newspaper editor at *The Balance and Columbian Repository* in Hudson, New York, defined a cocktail as "a stimulating liquor, composed of spirits of any kind, sugar, water, and bitters" (note that ice is not mentioned).[15] (Both the reader's query and the editor's reply are reproduced here.)

Communication.

To the Editor of the Balance.

Sir,

I observe in your paper of the 6th instant, in the account of a democratic candidate for a seat in the Legislature, marked under the head of Loss, 25 do. *cocktail.* Will you be so obliging as to inform me what is meant by this species of refreshment? Though a stranger to you, I believe, from your general character, you will not suppose this request to be impertinent.

[As I make it a point, never to publish any thing (under my editorial head) but what I can explain, I shall not hesitate to gratify the curiosity of my inquisitive correspondent:—*Cock-tail,* then, is a stimulating liquor, composed of *spirits* of any kind, *sugar, water,* and *bitters*—it is vulgarly called *bittered sling,* and is supposed to be an excellent electioneering potion, inasmuch as it renders the heart stout and bold, at the same time that it fuddles the head. It is said also, to be of great use to a democratic candidate: because, a person having swallowed a glass of it, is ready to swallow any thing else.

Edit. Bal.]

To put the timing of this definition in perspective, Thomas Jefferson was the president of the United States, George III was the king of Great Britain, and Napoleon I was the emperor of France. The original cocktail most likely included a domestic whiskey (rye grain was—and still is—grown in New York State and distilled into rye whiskey), as most other "stimulating liquor" would have been imported. The United States' largest trading partner in 1806 was Great Britain, which was trying to limit U.S. trade with France, eventually leading to the War of 1812. Because of this conflict, the United States relied as much as it could on domestically produced products, including whiskey. In addition, any imported liquor would have been much more expensive because of the import tax levied. At the time, import taxes were the U.S. government's only source of revenue; items produced in the United States were not taxed, and the permanent income tax did not take effect until after 1913, with passage of the Sixteenth Amendment to the Constitution.

In short, in all likelihood, the first cocktail was made in New York State with rye whiskey, bitters, sugar, and water and garnished with the tail feather of a rooster. The whiskey was of strong proof, as evidenced by the last two sentences of the newspaper editor's answer: a cocktail "is vulgarly called bitter sling, and is supposed to be an excellent electioneering potion, inasmuch as it renders the heart stout and bold, at the same time that it fuddles the head. It is said also, to be of great use to a democratic candidate: because, a person having swallowed a glass of it, is ready to swallow any thing else." In other words, the drink was so strong that it impaired the judgment of the person consuming it. The "democratic candidate" mentioned by the editor refers to the Democratic-Republican Party of Thomas Jefferson, which opposed the Federalist Party of Alexander Hamilton and John Adams. Jefferson opposed the tax on wine and considered that beverage infinitely preferable to whiskey:

> I rejoice as a moralist at the prospect of a reduction of the duties on wine, by our national legislature. It is an error to view a tax on that liquor as merely a tax on the rich. It is a prohibition of its use to the middling class of our citizens, and a condemnation of them to the poison of whiskey, which is desolating their houses. No nation is drunken where wine is cheap; and none sober, where the dearness of wine substitutes ardent spirits as the common beverage. It is, in truth, the only antidote to the bane of whiskey. Fix but the duty at the rate of other merchandise, and

we can drink wine here as cheap as grog; and who will not prefer it? Its extended use will carry health and comfort to a much enlarged circle. Everyone in easy circumstances (as the bulk of our citizens are) will prefer it to the poison to which they are now driven by their government. And the treasury itself will find that a penny apiece from a dozen is more than a groat from a single one. This reformation, however, will require time.[16]

Because whiskey was cheap and wine was expensive (as it was imported and thus taxed), whiskey had become the drink of the masses. And if the whiskey of the time had a harsh taste, some bitters, a little sugar, and water would go a long way toward making it palatable. This was even more important because ice—considered a luxury item and reserved for general refrigeration—would not have been wasted on a cocktail.

WHISKEY AS CURRENCY

Before 1792, whiskey was commonly used as currency in the United States by farmers. Whereas it would have been almost impossible for them to move a large crop to market—requiring a team of horses and a very large cart—the same crop distilled into whiskey required only one donkey to get it to market. In addition, farmers could use the whiskey they produced to purchase most of their necessities. The other option after 1775 was to trade with "pounds" issued by each individual state and denominated in Spanish dollars. Each state's currency (also known as continental currency) traded at a different rate, which meant that one state's currency might be stronger than another's. For example, early in this period, the currency of Georgia was worth more than six times that of South Carolina. In addition, whenever people traveled from one state to another, they would have to exchange their currency. Whiskey provided a strong, consistent currency and allowed exchange-free passage from state to state. The Coinage Act of 1792 established a formal currency for the United States, but for years after its passage, farmers still bartered their whiskey, as they always had. Many found that whiskey was a stronger "currency" than the early U.S. dollar. In fact, when Abraham Lincoln's family moved from Kentucky to Indiana in the early 1800s, his father, Thomas Lincoln, paid for the Indiana property in part in whiskey.

After the Revolutionary War, the United States found itself saddled with a huge war debt. In an attempt to raise funds to pay off the debt, Secretary of the Treasury Alexander Hamilton suggested that Congress pass a tax on whiskey. The so-called Whiskey Act, which became law in 1791, imposed the first tax by the U.S. government on a domestically produced product. It provided two ways for whiskey producers to pay the tax: a flat fee or by the gallon. The more whiskey a producer made, the less he paid per gallon. Some small distillers claimed this tax was designed to put them out of business in favor of large distillers. In addition, it acted as an income tax on farmers who were trying to move their crops to market without incurring the expense required to transport undistilled crops.

For the first eighteen months, the tax was largely uncollected. When the government moved to enforce the law, the farmers rebelled by tarring and feathering tax collectors. This became known as the Whiskey Rebellion. In July 1794 the conflict came to a climax when shots were exchanged at the Battle of Bower Hill. President George Washington, as the commander in chief, led 15,000 militia to put down the rebels, meeting minimal resistance. Several people were tried for treason, but none were put to death. (Washington is one of only two commanders in chief to lead an army into battle. The other was James Madison, who in 1814 led troops on a retreat from Washington, D.C., when the British burned the Capitol and the White House during the War of 1812.) The Whiskey Act was repealed in 1801, during the Jefferson administration and shortly before the cocktail was first mentioned in print. While whiskey was important as a currency up to 1792, it took on new significance upon repeal as a drink that could be produced and sold tax free, unlike wine.

ORIGINS OF THE OLD FASHIONED WHISKEY COCKTAIL

According to legend, the Old Fashioned was invented at the Pendennis Club in Louisville, Kentucky. Most people still believe this, and most of the literature reflects this perception. However, David Wondrich has busted this myth, pointing out that the drink was clearly mentioned in the *Chicago Tribune* a year before the Pendennis Club was founded in 1881.[17] I would argue that the Old Fashioned *as we know it today* (made with bourbon and muddled fruit) might have originated at the Pendennis Club. Regardless, the members of this private club in downtown Louisville have proudly adopted the Old Fashioned and given it a home.

When a member of the Pendennis Club asks for an Old Fashioned, the expectation is that the cocktail will be made with a seven-year-old bourbon whiskey. Although the original cocktail was made with rye whiskey, by the time this drink was ordered at the Pendennis Club, it was more than seventy-five years old—or "old-fashioned." The Kentucky bartender would have had greater access to bourbon and most likely substituted that for rye. This substitution created a new cocktail called the Old Fashioned.

DEFINING THE AUTHENTIC OLD FASHIONED WHISKEY COCKTAIL

Some of the first recipes, though similar, look different from the recipes of today. In 1885 *La Cuisine Creole* by Lafcadio Hearn featured several whiskey cocktails— including a New Orleans–style cocktail and a "spoon" cocktail—that contain all the components of an Old Fashioned except the cherry and the orange slice.[18] The difference between Hearn's two recipes is that the New Orleans–style cocktail is strained into a cocktail glass and has a choice of three bitters (Boker's, Angostura, or Peychaud), while the spoon cocktail demands Angostura bitters and is served "in small bar glass with spoon."[19] (After almost 110 years, we have advanced from a cock's feather to a proper spoon.) By 1895, this recipe appeared in the book *Modern American Drinks* by George J. Kappeler; although it is identical to the whiskey cocktail featured a decade earlier in *La Cuisine Creole*, it now sports the name Old Fashioned Whiskey Cocktail.[20] This simple drink bears little resemblance to the modern Old Fashioned, which has a slice of orange and a cherry. Kappeler confirms Angostura bitters as the type to use for an authentic Old Fashioned and goes a step further, making the distinction between the Old Fashioned Whiskey Cocktail and the Whiskey Cocktail. The latter introduces the cherry (not part of the original Old Fashioned), uses gum syrup (rather than sugar and water), and calls for more ice; there is no mention of leaving a spoon in the glass. Thus, it is safe to say at this point that the Whiskey Cocktail can use any bitters, while the Old Fashioned must contain Angostura bitters.

The Whiskey Cocktail listed in Jerry Thomas's *Bar-Tender's Guide*, published in 1887, is similar to Kappeler's. Thomas employs gum syrup and Boker's bitters to create his Whiskey Cocktail. Thomas also lists an "Improved Whiskey Cocktail" that calls for "bourbon or rye whiskey" and gives the reader the choice of "Boker's or Angostura Bitters," suggesting that bourbon (or rye) and Angostura bitters are upgrades from the well or house brands.[21] Haigh (Dr. Cocktail) draws the distinction between the two drinks in his book *Vintage Spirits and Forgotten Cocktails*: the Whiskey Cocktail may have curaçao added, most certainly has rye whiskey as its base, and is not garnished, while the Old Fashioned has no curaçao, uses bourbon or rye as its base, and is garnished with "a lone broad swathe of orange peel ONLY, muddled to express the orange oil."[22]

THE GLASS

The Old Fashioned Whiskey Cocktail should be served in a specific glass called, appropriately, the Old Fashioned glass (also known as a "rocks glass"). Not all cocktails have such a distinction; in fact, the Old Fashioned is one of the few. The Old Fashioned glass is perfect for any spirits or other alcoholic beverages served "on the rocks," or with ice.[23] It is also good for all sorts of mixed drinks, from Screwdrivers to Margaritas.[24] The Old Fashioned glass is round, short, and squat, with a thick bottom and an opening wide enough to allow one to enjoy the aroma of anything poured into it. The glass holds between 6 and 10 ounces.[25] There is also a double Old Fashioned glass that holds up to 12 ounces and is known for its heft.[26]

The Old Fashioned glass provides enough space to manipulate, crush, or stir the ingredients, and the bottom of the glass is built to withstand the force of muddling fruit, sugar, and bitters. There is enough room for a generous portion of liquid, ice, and fruit, and some bartenders finish the cocktail with soda water to make the glass look full.

In their book *The Bar: A Spirited Guide to Cocktail Alchemy*, Olivier Said and James Mellgren list the Old Fashioned glass as one of three pieces of "primary bar glassware" needed by the home mixologist; the other two are the Martini glass and the Highball or Collins glass. They note that the Old Fashioned glass is the best choice for serving spirits on the rocks.[27]

THE INGREDIENTS

Sugar and Water, or Simple Syrup

Originally, sugar was added to the Old Fashioned Whiskey Cocktail to make the drink palatable. In the early days of distilling in the United States, the alcohol produced was intoxicating but not very tasty. In addition, the whiskey was very high proof. The sugar

sweetened the flavor of the "hot" alcohol, cooling it for consumption. Today's whiskey is of the highest quality, so the sugar is now used to enhance the flavor of the whiskey. Water is added for no other reason than to dissolve the sugar. The finer the sugar, the more easily it dissolves; for this reason, the bartender or home drink maker should consider using castor sugar or superfine sugar. The authentic Old Fashioned calls for a sugar cube or sugar loaf, both of which require muddling to break up the sugar and allow it to dissolve into the drink.

David A. Embury, author of *The Fine Art of Mixing Drinks,* states that the only way to make a perfect Old Fashioned is to use simple syrup. He claims that water has no place in a cocktail and that it takes about twenty minutes to dissolve the sugar properly and completely, compared with only two minutes when using simple syrup.[28] Simple syrup—sometimes referred to as gum syrup—is easy to make and consists of equal portions of sugar and water boiled for at least three minutes to stabilize the solution in liquid form. Bartenders might also substitute other liquid sweeteners such as honey, maple syrup, agave syrup, or some other flavored syrup.[29]

BITTERS

Bitters are an infused, aromatic, distilled spirit (or glycerin) containing bittering compounds such as herbs, spices, roots, barks, flowers, peels, or seeds.[30]

Some are based on fruits, such as oranges, but they can also be made from rhubarb, saffron, sweet rush, and grapefruit. Bitters were originally produced to relax and sooth the stomach, which is why they are sometimes referred to as "digestives." Angostura bitters are required to create an authentic Old Fashioned. Dr. Johann Gottlieb Benjamin Siegert created Angostura bitters in 1824, after almost four years of experimentation. Siegert was a German expatriate in Venezuela when Simón Bolívar appointed him surgeon general for the military hospital in the town of Angostura. Siegert used his bitters as a natural remedy for Bolívar's forces, and in 1830 he started to promote his special blend for sale internationally. By the time of his death in 1870, he had established the reputation of Angostura bitters.

Many bartenders used to make their own bitters utilizing a variety of ingredients. While many bitters recipes are proprietary and are kept under lock and key, several examples can be found in pre-Prohibition cocktail books. Thomas lists this recipe for "Decanter Bitters" in his 1887 *Bar-Tender's Guide*:[31]

> ¼ pound of raisins
> 2 ounces of cinnamon
> 1 ounce of snake root
> 1 lemon and 1 orange cut in slices
> 1 ounce of cloves
> 1 ounce of all-spice
> Fill decanter with Santa Cruz rum.

As fast as the bitters is used fill up again with rum.

Parsons gives advice and lists thirteen recipes for making homemade bitters.[32]

Whiskey

Whiskey is the featured ingredient in the Old Fashioned, but not all whiskeys are made in the same manner with the same ingredients, nor do they all taste the same. In fact, producers don't even agree on the proper spelling of the word. In this book, I use the spelling *whiskey* throughout, except when referring to Scotch or Canadian *whisky* (although I concede that some bourbons are spelled *whisky,* such as Maker's Mark bourbon whisky). Recipes include different whiskeys based on availability or the author's personal preference. An Old Fashioned can be made with other distilled spirits such as brandy,[33] rum,[34] gin,[35] or tequila,[36] but most recipes feature whiskey. Some people have suggested that a "classic" Old Fashioned is made with blended Canadian whisky.[37] However, this seems to oppose logic, given the type of whiskey that was produced and available in the United States around the time the cocktail was created (unless a bartender referenced an old text that called for "rye whiskey" and misunderstood that to mean Canadian whisky). As for the Old Fashioned first made at the Pendennis Club, why would someone from Louisville, Kentucky, use an imported whisky (from another state or another country) to make a cocktail when there was so much bourbon available? In New York, why would someone use a taxed, imported whiskey when tax-free whiskey was available?

To create a traditional Old Fashioned, one might use bourbon whiskey, Tennessee whiskey, Canadian whisky, Irish whiskey, Scotch whisky, rye whiskey, grain whiskey, or corn whiskey. One might also consider Japanese whiskey or Indian whiskey for a twist on tradition. How do all these whiskeys differ?

BOURBON WHISKEY is a product of the United States. It is made from a minimum of 51 percent corn mash that is usually mixed with barley malt and either wheat or rye. Bourbon comes off the still at no more than 160 proof (80 percent alcohol by volume) and is cut with pure water, which is the only thing added to bourbon. The whiskey is placed in a new charred white oak barrel at no more than 125 proof (62.5 percent alcohol by volume), where it is aged. The addition of wheat or rye influences the overall flavor of the whiskey.

TENNESSEE WHISKEY is similar in formula to bourbon, but it must be made in the state of Tennessee and must include the Lincoln County process, which involves filtration through sugar maple charcoal. This gives Tennessee whiskey a unique flavor.

CANADIAN WHISKY is made from a neutral-grain spirit and rye whiskey (which might be why some people confuse Canadian whisky for rye whiskey and believe that Canadian whisky should be used to create an "authentic" Old Fashioned). Canadian whisky can be blended with other ingredients (constituting a little over 9 percent), such as sherry wine, fruit, or other whiskeys (some are blended with bourbon). Canadian whisky must be matured for three years and can be aged in used barrels.

IRISH WHISKEY is traditionally triple distilled and can be made from corn; however, if it is termed "pure pot still whiskey," it is made from both malted and raw barley. Triple distillation makes the resulting whiskey very smooth. Irish whiskey must be distilled in Ireland and matured for a minimum of three years.

SCOTCH WHISKY is made with malted barley and water in Scotland, distilled to a proof no higher than 189.6 (94.6 percent alcohol by volume), and aged in oak casks for at least three years. Also, the only thing that can be added to Scotch besides water is caramel coloring. Scotch whisky cannot be bottled at less than 80 proof (40 percent alcohol by volume).

RYE WHISKEY is made from not less than 51 percent rye grain and is aged in new charred oak barrels. To be labeled "straight rye," the whiskey must be aged for at least two years in barrels.

GRAIN WHISKEY is made from any grain or mixture of grains and is generally distilled in a continuous still.

CORN WHISKEY is made from a minimum of 80 percent corn and is less than 80 percent alcohol by volume (160 proof). This whiskey can be aged in used barrels, with no minimum maturation period specified.

JAPANESE WHISKEY is a mixture of malt and grain spirits made in Japan and based on a Scottish model. Like many other aspects of Japanese life and culture, the whiskey is made to exacting standards.

INDIAN WHISKEY is one of the remnants of the British Empire, but what qualifies as whiskey in India might not qualify as whiskey anywhere else. The Indians use buckwheat, rice, millet, or molasses, and according to Indian law, the whiskey does not need to be aged. Some whiskey produced in India does qualify to be labeled as whiskey in other countries.

GARNISH

Traditionally, the garnish for the Old Fashioned Whiskey Cocktail is a slice of orange or lemon peel that is twisted above the glass before being placed in

the drink. Over time, the citrus peel twist became an actual slice of orange (or, in some cases, both an orange slice and a lemon slice); the fruit is sometimes muddled in the drink, but it may be used just to garnish the rim of the glass. A maraschino cherry also garnishes this drink.

TO MUDDLE OR NOT TO MUDDLE?

One of the debates surrounding the Old Fashioned is whether the fruit should be muddled. Robert Hess, in *The Essential Bartender's Pocket Guide,* claims that muddling the fruit is a "fairly new addition to the drink" and warns that it "quite likely marks the beginning of the downfall" of the Old Fashioned.[38] In fact, most of the early recipes don't call for fruit at all—just a slice of lemon peel. Even the recipe used by the Waldorf=Astoria just after Prohibition calls for lemon peel.

David Embury, however, says that muddling makes the fruit flavors and liquors blend "exquisitely."[39] Jack Bettridge, writing in *Wine Spectator,* divides the Old Fashioned into the old (classic) Old Fashioned and the new Old Fashioned (the way people really drink it), based on muddling.[40] Professional bartenders or mixologists should ask their customers if they want the fruit muddled; at the very least, the menu should describe the customers' options. At home, you can make this cocktail however you like.

HAIR OF THE DOG

The Old Fashioned was originally consumed in the morning, as were other cocktails. The cocktail may have served the function of dealing with a hangover,

providing a little "hair of the dog." The idea is that when you wake up in the morning with a hangover, you drink a little of whatever you were drinking the night before to relieve the discomfort. Even if the

Old Fashioned was not specifically designed to treat a hangover, its creator included everything needed to do so: the whiskey helps take the edge off, the sugar helps raise blood-sugar levels, the bitters settle the stomach, and the citrus peel adds a pleasant aroma.

2

Places, People, and Things

THE PENDENNIS CLUB

The Pendennis Club is a private social club in Louisville, Kentucky, that opened in 1881. It moved to its current location in 1928 (during Prohibition) and is now on the National Historical Register. Old Forester bottles a seven-year-old private-label bourbon for the Pendennis Club. When someone at the club orders an Old Fashioned without specifying a whiskey preference, Old Forester is the well (default) whiskey. The club currently has 735 members. Even though it is club policy not to disclose the names of members, former club president Bill Wobee says the list reads like a who's who of the bourbon industry, in addition to social and community leaders. Most books and newspaper articles attribute the first Old Fashioned Whiskey Cocktail to an unnamed bartender at this club, who created the drink for a retired Civil War general.[1] Another creation claimed by the Pendennis Club is Henry Bain sauce.

THE WALDORF=ASTORIA HOTEL

The Waldorf=Astoria Hotel in New York started as two competing hotels owned by two different branches of the Astor family. William Waldorf Astor built the Waldorf in the late 1800s, and his cousin John Jacob Astor IV built the Astoria a few years later (and four stories higher). The two individual hotels were built side by side, highlighting the family feud. Eventually, the two structures were connected, and the resulting Waldorf=Astoria became the largest hotel in the world at the time. Colonel James E. Pepper, a member of the Pendennis Club, may have introduced the Old Fashioned Whiskey Cocktail to the Waldorf's "sit-down" bar, or the drink may have been created in his honor during one of Pepper's visits to New York.[2]

The Astor family feud was never resolved. William Waldorf Astor moved his family to Great Britain, where he opened a Waldorf Hotel in London's West End. Eventually, Astor was honored for his philanthropic contributions with a British peerage, becoming Baron Astor of Hever Castle and later Viscount

Astor. His namesake William Waldorf Astor, Fourth Viscount Astor, is an elected hereditary peer in the House of Lords, and many other descendants have served in both houses of Parliament.

John Jacob Astor IV was on the RMS *Titanic* when it sank in 1912. Astor held the distinction of being the richest passenger aboard. His body was recovered and is buried in Trinity Church Cemetery in New York City. His son, John Jacob Astor VI, was born after his death.

JAMES E. PEPPER

James Edward Pepper was born in Woodford County, Kentucky, on May 18, 1850, the son of General Oscar Pepper (could this be the unnamed Civil War general?) and Annette Edward. His grandfather was Elijah Pepper, the founder of "Old 1776" bourbon— its slogan was "Born with the Republic." James took over the family distillery (located at what is today the Woodford Reserve Distillery) when his father died in 1867. In 1870 James moved to New York and is remembered as having introduced the Old Fashioned Whiskey Cocktail to the bartender at the Old Waldorf Bar. Pepper was a member of the Pendennis Club and the Manhattan and New York Athletic Clubs, and he was twice president of the Lexington Union Club. In 1890 he married Ella Offutt. In addition to distilling, Pepper was a noted horse breeder: Mirage and The Dragon were Kentucky Derby contenders in 1893 and 1896, respectively, and Miss Dixie was the 1892 Kentucky Oaks champion. Pepper died in 1906, and the family sold the distillery in 1908.

BROADWAY

The Old Fashioned Whiskey Cocktail is featured in the 1940s Broadway musical *Panama Hattie*, music and lyrics by Cole Porter. Ironically, the singer asks for a double Old Fashioned without any garnish or bitters—that is, straight:

MAKE IT ANOTHER OLD-FASHIONED, PLEASE

*Since I went on the wagon, I'm certain drink is
    a major crime
For when you lay off the liquor, you feel so
    much slicker
Well that is, most of the time
But there are moments, sooner or later
When it's tough, I got to say, love to say . . . Waiter*

Make it another old-fashioned, please
Make it another, double, old-fashioned, please
Make it for one who's due to join the
    disillusion crew
Make it for one of love's new refugees

Once high in my castle, I ran to you
And oh what a castle, built on a
    heavenly dream
Then quick as a lightning flash, that castle
    began to crash
So, make it another old-fashioned, please

Leave out the cherry,
Leave out the orange,
Leave out the bitters
Just make it straight, right

WALLACE IRWIN'S
"THE GREAT AMERICAN COCKTAIL"

Wallace Irwin was an American who wrote novels, short stories, screenplays, and poems, often using pseudonyms. He was born in New York and lived in Colorado and California before passing away in North

Carolina just before his eighty-fourth birthday. One of his poems, "The Great American Cocktail," was first published in 1902 in the *San Francisco News Letter*.[3] It also appeared four years later in *The Book of Spice* by "Ginger." In the middle of the poem Irwin discusses the elements of a cocktail. Although he never mentions the Old Fashioned by name, in eight lines he manages to reference almost every element of it, including the whiskey, the bitters, the orange peel (in the 1902 version it's "lemon peel," which still works), and the cherry.

> Perhaps it's made of whiskey and perhaps it's made of gin, perhaps there's orange bitters and an orange-peel within, perhaps it's called Martini and perhaps it's called again, the name that spread Manhattan's fame among the sons of men; perhaps you like it garnished with what thinking men avoid, the little blushing cherry that is made of celluloid, but be these matters as they may, a cher confrere you are if you admire the cocktail they pass along the bar.[4]

THE SAT

Kurt Reighley, in his book *United States of Americana*, points out, "If you took the SAT exams back

in the twentieth century, you may recall the curious puzzle 'Salt is to food, as bitters are to [blank].'
What scholar had the bright idea that high school
juniors knew how to mix a proper old-fashioned
anyway?"[5]

3

Recipes

Here are some tips for making the perfect authentic Old Fashioned Whiskey Cocktail:

1. Make each drink individually.
2. Use an Old Fashioned glass.
3. Use a teaspoon of castor sugar or a sugar cube (or simple syrup).
4. Use just a little hot water.
5. Use Angostura bitters, and muddle the sugar water and bitters until well blended.
6. Don't muddle the fruit; use it only as a garnish.
7. Use bourbon (high proof).
8. Cut a large strip of orange peel, and twist it over the glass.
9. Use as few ice cubes as possible.

SIR KINGSLEY AMIS'S BOURBON OLD FASHIONED

Sir Kingsley Amis, CBE (1922–1995), was many things during his life: the writer of more than twenty books, including the James Bond novel Colonel Sun *(written under the pseudonym Robert Markham); a teacher; and an alcoholic beverage expert. Amis believed that "you really have to use bourbon" when making the Old Fashioned.[1] Olivier Said and James Mellgren concur, including the Old Fashioned in a short list of cocktails that use bourbon as the base spirit.[2] Sheree Bykofsky and Megan Buckley, authors of* Sexy City Cocktails, *point out that since the whiskey is in the "spotlight," you will want to use "the best bourbon you can find."[3] Amis believed that the Old Fashioned could not be mass-produced successfully, so each drink should be mixed individually.[4] He used the fruit as a garnish and did not muddle.*

1 level teaspoon castor sugar
Hot water—just enough to dissolve the sugar completely
3 dashes Angostura bitters
1 hefty squeeze fresh orange juice
1 teaspoon maraschino cherry juice
1 huge slug (about 4 fluid ounces) bourbon whiskey
3 ice cubes
1 orange slice
1 maraschino cherry

Put the dissolved sugar in a glass; add the bitters, orange and cherry juices, and whiskey; stir furiously. Add the ice cubes and stir again. Push the orange slice down alongside the ice, drop in the cherry, and serve. Supply drinking straws, if it's that sort of party.

CANADIAN WHISKY OLD FASHIONED

Williams-Sonoma's The Bar Guide *recounts the story of the Old Fashioned Whiskey Cocktail's creation at the Pendennis Club in the late 1880s.*[5] *It concedes that the first Old Fashioned was most likely made with bourbon but states that blended Canadian whisky is now the ingredient of choice. This recipe suggests muddling the fruit.*

3 dashes Angostura bitters
1 orange slice
1 lemon wedge
1 maraschino cherry
1 sugar cube
Ice cubes
2½ fluid ounces (75 mL) blended Canadian whisky

Put the bitters, orange slice, lemon wedge, maraschino cherry, and sugar cube in an Old Fashioned glass and muddle well. Fill the glass with ice cubes. Add the whisky. Stir well.

IRISH WHISKEY OLD FASHIONED

The use of Irish Whiskey for an Old Fashioned is outlined in Williams-Sonoma's The Bar Guide.[6] *I have always referred to Irish whiskey as a "gateway" whiskey for my students who prefer vodka, because of its approachably smooth flavor. The fruit is muddled in this recipe.*

3 dashes Angostura bitters
1 orange slice
1 lemon wedge
1 maraschino cherry
1 sugar cube
Ice cubes
2½ fluid ounces (75 mL) Irish whiskey

Put the bitters, orange slice, lemon wedge, maraschino cherry, and sugar cube in an Old Fashioned glass and muddle well. Fill the glass with ice cubes. Add the whiskey. Stir well.

RYE OLD FASHIONED

I found this recipe in The Savoy Food and Drink Book, *featuring an introduction by Kingsley Amis.*[7] *Sir Kingsley declared that the rye Old Fashioned was "not too bad."*[8] *This recipe features the fruit as a garnish (no muddling) and adds a lemon peel twist to the mix.*

1 lump, or 1 teaspoon, sugar
2 dashes Angostura bitters
2 fluid ounces rye whiskey
1 ice cube
1 lemon peel twist
1 orange slice
1 maraschino cherry

Crush the sugar and bitters together in a medium-sized glass. Add the whiskey and the ice cube, and decorate with the lemon peel, orange slice, and maraschino cherry. This cocktail can also be made with other spirits.

SCOTCH OLD FASHIONED

The Scotch Old Fashioned was described by Sir Kingsley Amis as "not worth while,"[9] but New Orleans restaurant legend Ella Brennan disagrees; according to Ti Martin and Lally Brennan, the Scotch Old Fashioned is her drink of choice.[10] This recipe appears in David Renton's Dorchester Cocktail Book, *where it leads the chapter titled "Pre-Dinner Cocktails."[11] Renton's book has many useful recipes, including classic cocktails, original creations, and a section on canapés. He suggests using the fruit as a garnish only—no muddling. It is important to note that Renton uses the word* measure *to express the amount of whisky used. He explains that because different people like different-sized drinks, you can choose any measuring cup or glass and use the same amount each time in relation to the other ingredients.[12] Japanese whiskey and Indian whiskey can be substituted, with similar results.*

3 dashes Angostura bitters
1 lump sugar
Water
Ice cubes
1 measure Scotch whisky
1 orange slice
1 maraschino cherry

Pour the bitters onto the sugar in an Old Fashioned glass, dissolve with a little water, add ice, and pour the whisky. Decorate with the orange slice and cherry.

TENNESSEE WHISKEY OLD FASHIONED

Jack Daniel's is one of three companies making Tennessee whiskey, but it is the only one owned by Louisville-based Brown-Forman. This is the company's standard recipe, featured in both Jack Daniel's Cookbook: The Spirit of Tennessee *and* Jack Daniel's Old Time Barbecue Cookbook.[13]

Pinch sugar, dissolved in ½ teaspoon water
2 drops bitters
1 orange slice, halved
1 maraschino cherry
Jack Daniel's whiskey

Combine the first four ingredients in an Old Fashioned glass. Top with Jack Daniel's whiskey to taste.

HISTORICAL OLD FASHIONED WHISKEY COCKTAILS AND OTHER BEVERAGES

WHISKEY, BRANDY, OR GIN COCKTAIL
NEW ORLEANS STYLE

Even though Lafcadio Hearn doesn't call this an Old Fashioned Whiskey Cocktail, there is a striking resemblance to other early recipes. This drink is from Hearn's La Cuisine Creole, *published in 1885:*

> Two dashes of Boker's, Angostura or Peychaud bitters—either will make a fine cocktail. One lump of sugar, one-piece of lemon peel, one tablespoon of water, one wineglassful of liquor, etc., with plenty of ice. Stir well and strain into a cocktail glass.[14]

ROYAL COCKTAIL (MORAN'S OWN)

Here is another cocktail from Hearn:

> One lump of sugar; two dashes of Boker's bitters or Angostura bitters; two tablespoonfuls of Belfast ginger ale; one wineglassful of whiskey or brandy; one lemon peel; plenty of ice. Shake well, and strain in fancy glass.[15]

MINT JULEP

Note the absence of bitters, distinguishing a julep from a cocktail:

> One half tablespoonful of powdered sugar, one wineglass of water, one of whiskey, brandy or gin, etc., and one half dozen sprigs of mint. Use plenty of fine ice, and decorate with strawberries and pineapples, or any fruit in season.[16]

NEW ORLEANS TODDY

> One lump sugar, one tablespoonful of water, one wineglassful of whiskey or brandy, one lump of ice. Use small bar glass.[17]

THE OLD FASHIONED WHISKEY COCKTAIL

This recipe is from George Kappeler's Modern American Drinks, *published in 1895:*

> Dissolve a small lump of sugar with a little water in a whiskey-glass; add two dashes Angostura bitters, a small piece ice, a piece lemon-peel, one jigger whiskey. Mix with small bar-spoon and serve, leaving spoon in glass.[18]

THE WHISKEY COCKTAIL

Contrast this recipe of Kappeler's with the one above:

> Mixing-glass half-full fine ice, two dashes gum-syrup, two dashes Angostura or Peychaud bitters, one jigger whiskey. Mix, strain into cocktail-glass; add a small piece of twisted lemon-peel or a cherry.[19]

In 1917, when Thomas Bullock penned his book *The Ideal Bartender,*[20] Congress had already proposed the Eighteenth Amendment to the Constitution. When it was ratified in 1919, this amendment prohibited people in the United States from "producing, transporting and selling" alcohol; the Volstead Act was passed the same year to enforce these provisions. Consumption was not limited, however, which meant that the demand for alcohol was unchanged, but there was no (legal) supply. Canada also experienced a prohibition on alcohol, but it lasted for only one year, compared with more than thirteen years in the United States. When the Twenty-first Amendment was proposed in 1933, it took less than eleven months for Congress to pass it and for two-thirds of the states to ratify it, resulting in the repeal of Prohibition.

The following recipe from Bullock has several interesting elements:

1. The drink is called the "Old Fashion Cocktail," not the Old Fashioned Whiskey Cocktail.
2. The recipe specifies bourbon as opposed to another whiskey or a choice of whiskeys.
3. There is no cherry or orange, but there is lemon skin.
4. A toddy glass is used instead of an Old Fashioned glass.

Also of note is that Bullock used to work at the Pendennis Club before moving to the St. Louis Country Club and that the introduction to *The Ideal Bartender* is authored by the future president of the United States Golf Association, George Herbert Walker (for whom the Walker Cup is named), the grandfather and namesake of the forty-first president of the United States, George Herbert Walker Bush.

THOMAS BULLOCK'S OLD FASHION COCKTAIL

Use a toddy glass.

1 lump ice
2 dashes Angostura bitters
1 lump sugar, dissolved in water
1½ jiggers bourbon whiskey

Twist a piece of lemon skin over the drink and drop it in. Stir well and serve.

ESQUIRE'S OLD FASHIONED DUTCH OR OLD FASHIONED GIN COCKTAIL

In 1933 Utah voted to ratify the Twenty-first Amendment, thus reaching the two-thirds majority needed to repeal Prohibition. By the end of the year, legal liquor started flowing again. Esquire magazine wasted no time issuing a "Top Ten Cocktail" list for 1934, which included the "Old Fashioned Dutch." [21] *Note that this cocktail is similar to early versions of the Old Fashioned Whiskey Cocktail, with no fruit. When an Old Fashioned is made with yellow gin, it is referred to as a Golden Spike.* [22]

1 sugar cube
2 dashes Angostura bitters
1 teaspoon water
2 ounces gin
2 large ice cubes

Place the sugar in an Old Fashioned glass or other smallish, heavy-bottomed tumbler. Add the bitters and water, and muddle the sugar until it dissolves. Add the gin—Genever or London Dry. Stir well, and add the ice cubes. Let it sit for a couple of minutes, and then have at it.[23]

THE OLD WALDORF BAR
OLD FASHIONED WHISKEY COCKTAIL

This drink was introduced to the Waldorf in the days of its sit-down bar by (or in honor of) Colonel James E. Pepper of Kentucky, the proprietor of a whiskey distillery and a member of the famous Pendennis Club in Louisville.

¼ lump sugar
2 spoons water
1 jigger whiskey
1 piece lemon peel
1 lump ice

Serve with a small spoon.[24]

IRVIN S. COBB'S
OLD FASHIONED WHISKEY COCKTAIL

Irvin S. Cobb, a native of Paducah, Kentucky, became a legend in his own time. Cobb was a writer and humorist of the highest order, and some of his stories were made into Hollywood films. Cobb took up acting and eventually hosted the Seventh Academy Awards ceremony, where Shirley Temple received the Academy's Juvenile Award. The following recipe is from Irvin S. Cobb's Own Recipe Book, *where he mentions that the Old Fashioned was created at the Pendennis Club "in Louisville in honor of a famous old-fashioned Kentucky Colonel."*[25]

½ piece sugar

2 dashes Angostura bitters

1 ice cube

1½ jiggers Paul Jones or Four Roses whiskey

2 dashes curaçao

1 slice orange

1 slice lemon

1 slice pineapple

Muddle the sugar and bitters with a pestle. Add the ice cube, whiskey, and curaçao, and decorate with fruit.

MARION FLEXNER'S OLD FASHIONED

Marion Flexner's Old Fashioned recipe in Out of Kentucky Kitchens *(which features an introduction by Duncan Hines, who was a native of Bowling Green, Kentucky) mentions Irvin S. Cobb (see above).*[26] *This recipe also suggests a connection between the Old Fashioned and the Kentucky Whiskey Toddy:*

> To the Kentucky Whiskey Toddy add a dash of Angostura bitters, a slice of lemon, half a slice of orange and a maraschino cherry.

MARION FLEXNER'S KENTUCKY WHISKEY TODDY

½ teaspoon sugar (or 1 teaspoon, if you have a
    sweet tooth)
1 tablespoon tap water (or more if you like a
    mild drink)
1 spilling jigger bourbon whiskey
Crushed ice or 2 ice cubes

Mix the sugar and water. Add the whiskey. Pour into an Old Fashioned glass and fill with crushed ice or add ice cubes. Stir until chilled. Serve.

PENDENNIS OLD FASHIONED COCKTAIL

Using an old-fashioned glass, crush a small lump of sugar in just enough water to dissolve thoroughly. Add one dash of Angostura and two dashes of orange bitters. Add large cube of ice and one jigger of whiskey. Twist and drop in lemon peel, and stir until mixed thoroughly. Remove ice and garnish with cherry.[27]

THE CLASSIC OLD FASHIONED

COLONEL MASTERS'S BOURBON OLD FASHIONED

Colonels and Kentucky seem to go together. This perception was solidified by Colonel Harland Sanders of Kentucky Fried Chicken fame. Another colonel from Kentucky, Michael Edward Masters (aka the Host of Kentucky), describes how to make an Old Fashioned with bourbon—as if there is a choice for a Kentucky colonel—in his book Hospitality Kentucky Style. *Masters ties the Old Fashioned to the toddy, explaining how to adapt the toddy recipe to turn it into an Old Fashioned:*

Pack crushed ice into an old-fashioned or tumbler glass. Add a teaspoon of sugar, a dash of Angostura Bitters, a maraschino cherry, and fine aged Kentucky bourbon whiskey. Place a slice of lemon and orange on the rim of the glass.[28]

GARY REGAN'S OLD FASHIONED

Gary Regan is a bartender, a consultant, and the author of several books, including The Bartender's Bible.[29] *He lists three recipes for the Old Fashioned that are identical, with the exception of the whiskey: one is made with bourbon, one with Scotch, and one with blended Canadian whisky. Regan suggests that Canadian whisky is the proper choice for a classic Old Fashioned.*

3 dashes bitters
1 teaspoon water
1 sugar cube
Ice cubes
3 ounces whiskey (bourbon, Scotch, or blended
    Canadian whisky)
1 orange slice
1 maraschino cherry

In an Old Fashioned glass, muddle the bitters and water into the sugar cube, using the back of a tea-spoon. Almost fill the glass with ice cubes, and add the whiskey. Garnish with the orange slice and cherry. Serve with a swizzle stick.

ROBERT HESS'S OLD FASHIONED

Robert Hess is the creator of www.drinkboy.com, one of the founders of the Museum of the American Cocktail, and the host and executive producer of The Cocktail Spirit, *a Web-based video series on the Small Screen Network. He is also the author of* The Essential Bartender's Pocket Guide.[30] *Here is his version of the Old Fashioned:*

1 sugar cube
1 teaspoon water
2 dashes Angostura bitters
Ice cubes
2 ounces American rye or bourbon whiskey
1 twist orange peel
1 maraschino cherry

Muddle the sugar, water, and bitters together until the sugar is mostly dissolved. Fill the glass with ice, and then add the whiskey. Stir briefly to chill. Garnish with the orange peel and cherry. Serve with straws.

THE DRINKS BIBLE OLD FASHIONED

1 teaspoon sugar
2 dashes Angostura bitters
1 orange wheel
1 maraschino cherry
2 ounces whiskey
Ice
Splash soda water

In a chilled Old Fashioned glass, muddle the sugar, bitters, orange wheel, and cherry until the sugar is dissolved. Add the whiskey, ice, and soda water and stir. Optional: garnish with a lemon twist.[31]

THE MODERN OLD FASHIONED

The idea that there is only one recipe for the Old Fashioned or that it should look a particular way is debunked by Brad Parsons, who points out, "The simplicity of the old-fashioned means that it lends itself to multiple variations."[32] Here are some of the modern variations that have been created by bartenders from around the world.

NEW OLD FASHIONED

The Internet has changed many aspects of life, including how we find recipes. The following recipe comes from www.about.com and substitutes peach slices for orange slices and blackberries for cherries.

1 tablespoon simple syrup
5 dashes bitters
2 peach slices
2½ ounces Woodford Reserve bourbon whiskey
Ice cubes
2 blackberries
Splash sparkling water

Muddle the simple syrup, bitters, and one peach slice in the bottom of an Old Fashioned glass. Add the bourbon, ice cubes, remaining peach slice, blackberries, and sparkling water. Stir and combine.

NEW WISCONSIN-STYLE OLD FASHIONED, OR BRANDY OLD FASHIONED

Another "new" Old Fashioned is made "Wisconsin style," or with brandy. This recipe comes from www .drinkoftheweek.com, which claims that this drink is more popular than cheese in Wisconsin.

2 ounces brandy
Dash Angostura bitters
3 ounces Squirt or grapefruit soda
Ice
1 maraschino cherry
Lemon and orange slices for garnish

Mix the first three ingredients with ice in an Old Fashioned (rocks) glass. Add cherry and garnish.

TRADITIONAL ELDERFASHIONED

This recipe comes from an advertisement for St.-Germain liqueur. The ad calls this drink one part tradition, one part refinement, and one part Bukowski—referring to Charles Bukowski, a German-born American poet and writer.

½ part St.-Germain
2 parts bourbon or straight rye whiskey
2 dashes Angostura bitters
Ice
Orange twist

Stir the ingredients into an Old Fashioned glass, add ice, and stir again as if you are a revolutionary. Add an orange twist and think progressively as you sip this new twist on a classic. Vive la Résistance!

The next three recipes were featured in Alison Miller's December 2011 article "5 Bottles, 25 Drinks, One Happy Holiday" in *Spirit: Southwest Airlines Magazine*. Of the twenty-five drinks, three were Old Fashioneds, and one was an "improved" cocktail that shares many of the elements of the Old Fashioned. The recipes were gleaned from a number of expert and experienced bartenders.

BOLS GENEVER OLD FASHIONED

Jeff Hollinger is identified as the "saloon keeper" of Comstock Saloon in San Francisco, California. Here is his recipe:

1 sugar cube
1 ounce water
1 large lemon peel
3 dashes Jerry Thomas's Own Decanter Bitters by
    The Bitter Truth
2½ ounces Bols genever
Ice cubes

Muddle the sugar cube, water, lemon peel, and bitters in a double Old Fashioned glass. Add the genever and fill with several large ice cubes. Stir until well chilled.

VIOLET OLD FASHIONED

Anu Apte, co-owner of Rob Roy, a craft-cocktail bar in Seattle, Washington, contributed this recipe:

2 ounces rye whiskey
½ ounce crème de violette
3 dashes Angostura bitters
1 large ice ball or cube
1 brandied cherry

Combine all the liquid ingredients in a mixing glass. Stir and strain into a double Old Fashioned glass over ice. Garnish with the brandied cherry.

OAXACA OLD FASHIONED

Phil Ward is the co-owner of Mayahuel in New York City. He recommends the following:

1½ ounces El Tesoro reposado tequila
½ ounce Del Maguey Vida mescal
1 teaspoon amber agave nectar
2 dashes Angostura bitters
Ice
1 orange twist

Combine the liquid ingredients in a mixing glass. Add ice, stir, and strain into a rocks glass over ice. Garnish with a flamed orange twist.

RUM OLD FASHIONED

This Old Fashioned is featured in Classic Cocktails from around the World *by Allan Gage.*[33] *It hails from La Bodega in Cairo, Egypt, where it is made with local rum. Gage writes that the 1920s-themed restaurant and bar is hard to find but worth the search. La Bodega is filled with local and foreign art, has a romantic view of the Nile, and features great classic cocktails.*

Dash Angostura bitters
Dash lime bitters
1 teaspoon castor sugar
½ measure water
3 ice cubes
2 measures white rum
½ measure dark rum
Lime twist

Stir the bitters, sugar, and water in the bottom of a heavy-based rocks glass with 1 ice cube until the sugar dissolves. Add the white rum, stir, and add 2 more ice cubes. Add the dark rum, and stir again. Decorate with a lime twist.

BLACKBERRY HONEY OLD FASHIONED

This drink comes from Louisville bartender Kiersten Gillam. She replaces the cherries and sugar with blackberries and honey. It is important to note that honey is sweeter than sugar, so less is required to achieve the same level of sweetness.

½ orange slice
2 blackberries
¼ teaspoon (a drizzle) of honey
2 dashes Gary Regan's orange bitters
Ice
1½ ounces bourbon whiskey
Soda to fill

In an Old Fashioned glass, muddle the orange slice, blackberries, honey, and bitters. Then fill the glass with ice, bourbon, and soda. Shake the ingredients together, strain the mixture into another glass over ice, and serve.

COMFORTABLY OLD FASHIONED

The Comfortably Old Fashioned comes from Lu Brow, the bartender at the Swizzle Stick Bar at Café Adelaide in New Orleans. This recipe was featured in The American Cocktail *by the editors of* Imbibe *magazine.*[34]

1 orange wheel, halved
½ bar spoon granulated sugar
2 dashes Angostura bitters
2 ounces Southern Comfort
Ice chunk
1 brandied cherry (see below)

Muddle the orange wheel, sugar, and bitters in an Old Fashioned glass. Add the Southern Comfort and stir. Add a large chunk of ice and garnish with a brandied cherry.

LU'S BRANDIED CHERRIES

Here is Lu Brow's recipe for brandying cherries.

1 pound sweet cherries
½ cup granulated sugar
½ cup water
2 teaspoons fresh lemon juice
1 cinnamon stick
Pinch freshly grated nutmeg
1 teaspoon pure vanilla extract
1 cup brandy

Wash and pit the cherries. In a small saucepan, combine the sugar, water, lemon juice, cinnamon stick, nutmeg, and vanilla and bring to a rolling boil. Reduce the heat to medium, add the cherries, and simmer for 5 to 7 minutes. Remove from the heat, stir in the brandy, and let cool. Transfer the cherries and their cooking liquid to a clean jar and refrigerate, uncovered, until the cherries are cool to the touch. Cover tightly and refrigerate for up to 2 weeks.

OLD FASHIONED GRANITA

Brad Parsons offers up this twist on the Old Fashioned in his book Bitters.[35] *He points out that the dessert is easy to make, since the freezer does most of the work. Just make sure to break up the ice crystals every 30 minutes. This recipe makes 4 to 6 servings.*

2 cups water
2 cups Demerara or turbinado sugar
1 cinnamon stick
1 tablespoon grated orange zest
1 tablespoon freshly squeezed orange juice
3 tablespoons bourbon
2 teaspoons Angostura bitters
1 teaspoon cherry juice
4–6 thick strips orange zest

Place a 9- by 13-inch glass or metal pan in the freezer to chill while you prepare the granita.

Combine the water and sugar in a saucepan over medium heat and stir until the sugar is completely dissolved. When it comes to a boil, remove from the heat and stir in the cinnamon stick, orange zest, orange juice, bourbon, bitters, and cherry juice. Let cool to room temperature.

Strain the mixture into the chilled pan and return to the freezer. After 30 minutes, stir the mixture with a whisk. Return the pan to the freezer for at least 3 hours, removing it every 30 minutes or so to scrape the ice crystals with a fork to break them up. You can leave the mixture chunky and crunchy, or break up the ice crystals more thoroughly for a softer, snow-ball-like consistency. Just before serving, give the granita one last fluff with a fork. Serve in short rocks glasses or Old Fashioned glasses garnished with strips of orange zest.

GRAND FASHIONED

Jason Kosmas and Dushan Zaric feature three Old Fashioneds in their book Speakeasy.[36] *The Grand Fashioned is made with Grand Marnier as a substitute for whiskey.*

1 teaspoon superfine sugar
3 dashes Angostura bitters
3 blood orange wedges, peeled
2 ounces Grand Marnier
¾ ounce freshly squeezed lime juice
Ice cubes

Muddle the sugar, bitters, and oranges in the bottom of a mixing glass. Add the Grand Marnier and lime juice. Add enough large ice cubes to fit in a rocks glass and shake vigorously but briefly. Pour the unstrained liquid into a rocks glass and serve.

JONATHAN'S OLD FASHIONED

Jonathan Lundy is the owner and executive chef at Jonathan at Gratz Park in Lexington, Kentucky. The native of Midway, Kentucky, has an impressive culinary pedigree, including an apprenticeship with chef Emeril Lagasse and a degree from Johnson and Wales University. His book Jonathan's Bluegrass Table *includes many of the recipes featured at his restaurant, along with his own interpretation of the Old Fashioned.*[37] *Note that he uses a specific bourbon—Maker's Mark (one of the bourbons that uses the Scottish spelling of* whisky*).*

2 Old Fashioned Macerated Cherries (see below)
1 slice navel orange, cut into half-moons
2 tablespoons juice from Old Fashioned Macerated
    Cherries (see below)
3–4 dashes Angostura bitters
Ice
3 ounces Maker's Mark Kentucky straight bourbon
    whisky
Splash ginger ale

In a large cocktail glass, muddle together the macerated cherries, 1 half-moon of navel orange, juice from the macerated cherries, and Angostura bitters. Fill the glass with ice and pour in the whisky. Stir to incorporate the ingredients. Top with ginger ale.

OLD FASHIONED MACERATED CHERRIES

Chef Lundy suggests using only fresh cherries for this recipe.[38]

2 cups sugar
2 tablespoons bourbon
½ cup Grand Marnier
2 tablespoons honey
2 pounds fresh cherries, washed and pitted
    (about 5 cups)

Place the sugar, bourbon, Grand Marnier, and honey in a medium-sized pot. Bring to a boil on high heat. Reduce heat and simmer for 5 minutes. Add the pitted cherries. Simmer for 5 minutes more. Remove from heat. Allow the cherries to cool at room temperature. Store in the refrigerator for up to 2 weeks.

SAID AND MELLGREN'S OLD FASHIONED

As mentioned earlier, Olivier Said and James Mellgren are of the opinion that bourbon should be used to create an Old Fashioned, but in this recipe from The Bar, *they call for either blended whiskey or bourbon.*[39]

½ teaspoon superfine sugar or 1 sugar cube
2 dashes Angostura bitters
½ orange slice
1 maraschino cherry
1½ ounces whiskey (either blended whiskey
    or bourbon)
Ice
Club soda to fill

Place the sugar in an Old Fashioned glass and shake the bitters on top of it. Add the orange slice and cherry and mash strongly with a muddler or the back of a spoon. Add the whiskey, fill with ice, and then fill with club soda.

PAPPY OLD FASHIONED

Scott Beattie, author of Artisanal Cocktails, *prefers to use a well-aged bourbon when making an Old Fashioned, but as he states in his book, very few bourbons are fifteen years or older.*[40] *Beattie uses a limited release of fifteen-year-old bourbon from the Van Winkle family, multiple bitters, and imported Italian cherries for this version of the Old Fashioned.*

1 sugar cube
2 dashes Angostura bitters
2 dashes orange bitters
½ orange slice
3 Amarena cherries
½ ounce seltzer
2 ounces Pappy Van Winkle's bourbon
Ice

Place the sugar cube in the bottom of a mixing glass and douse it with the bitters. Toss in the orange slice, one of the cherries, and the seltzer, and muddle it down. Add the bourbon and stir well. Add enough ice to fill the mixing glass half full, and stir a few times to mix. Pour the drink into a short (7 to 8 ounce) Old Fashioned glass to serve. Garnish with the remaining Amarena cherries skewered on a pick.

MINT NEW FASHIONED

Earlier, I suggested that the Mint Julep may have been adapted from the Old Fashioned. Here is a new twist on that idea.

6 mint leaves
½ tablespoon simple syrup
Ice
3 tablespoons rye or bourbon
1 tablespoon orange bitters

Place the mint leaves in a rocks glass and top with simple syrup. Use a muddler to bruise the mint leaves to release the oils. Fill the glass with ice and pour in the rye or bourbon and bitters. Gently stir and serve.

NEW FASHIONED

This recipe was created by mixologist Xavier Herit and is featured in the book Cocktails and Amuse-Bouches, *cowritten with chef Daniel Boulud.*[41] *This drink's unique presentation gives the concept of "rocks" a whole new meaning. Make sure to start this recipe a day ahead of time if you want to serve it at a party.*

Filtered water
Ice cubes
1½ ounces 100-proof rye, such as Rittenhouse
¾ ounce vermouth, preferably Carpano Punt e Mes
¼ ounce maple syrup
8 drops peach bitters
4 drops Peychaud bitters
1 orange peel
1 lemon peel

Clean the inside of a latex balloon. Fill the balloon with enough filtered water to fit in a cocktail glass; tie to close. Place the balloon in the freezer, suspended, so that nothing touches it and it keeps its shape. Freeze until frozen. Remove the balloon from the ice ball and discard; keep the ice ball frozen until ready to use.

Fill a large glass with ice cubes. Add the rye, vermouth, maple syrup, and both bitters; stir to combine. Strain into a rocks glass and add the ice ball; garnish with orange and lemon peels. Serve.

ANOTHER NEW FASHIONED

1 ounce Canadian whisky
½ ounce amaretto
¼ ounce simple syrup
3 dashes bitters
Ice
1 piece orange peel

Stir the liquid ingredients in a shaker with ice. Strain into a rocks glass. Serve chilled, neat, and garnished with the orange peel.

DICKIE BRENNAN'S OLD FASHIONED

This Old Fashioned holds a special place in my heart because it combines some wonderful memories from three different parts of the country: New Orleans, Kentucky, and Connecticut. The Dickie Brennan Bourbon House in New Orleans, located on Bourbon Street, features this recipe (and the one for the New Fashioned that follows) on its website, www.chefslagniappe.com. The lagniappe *(pronounced* lan-yap*) in the website's name refers to the tradition of giving something extra (a gift) to the customer (such as the thirteenth donut in a baker's do*ʒ*en). The website lives up to its name, offering some wonderful recipes. This Old Fashioned features Old Charter bourbon, which is made in Kentucky and refers to the charter oak tree,* *featured on the back of the Connecticut quarter issued by the U.S. Mint in 1999. It is also reminiscent of my alma mater, Charter Oak State College.*

1 splash simple syrup
2 dashes Peychaud bitters
1 maraschino cherry
1 orange slice
2 ounces Old Charter bourbon
Ice

Combine the simple syrup, bitters, cherry, and orange in an Old Fashioned glass. Muddle into a paste with the back of a spoon. Add bourbon, fill with ice, and stir.

DICKIE BRENNAN'S NEW FASHIONED

2 ounces macerated fruit
5 shakes Peychaud bitters
1 splash simple syrup
1 splash soda
2 ounces Knob Creek bourbon
Ice

Combine the macerated fruit (fruit that has been marinated in its own juices, with a touch of sugar, overnight), bitters, simple syrup, and soda in a rocks glass and muddle. Add the bourbon, fill with ice, and mix well.

YOUR OWN OLD FASHIONED

Fill in the blanks to make an Old Fashioned that suits your own personal tastes.

_____ sugar cubes
_____ water
_____ dashes Angostura bitters
_____ ice cubes
_____ ounces _____ whiskey or
_____ [another liquor]
_____ slice orange or _____
[another citrus fruit]
_____ cherries

Place the sugar in an Old Fashioned glass. Add the water and dissolve the sugar. Add the bitters, mix, and top with ice cubes. Add the whiskey, mix well, and garnish with fruit.

Acknowledgments

Many people contributed to the completion of this book. First and foremost I would like to thank my wife, Kimberly; my sons, Thomas and Michael; my parents, Thomas and Elizabeth Schmid; and my Kentucky parents, Richard and Carol Dunn, for their love and support.

Thanks are also due to the following people for their direct or indirect support of this project:

My brother and sisters and their spouses: Gretchen, Tiffany, Rachel, Justin, Bennett, Ana, Shane, and John. I always enjoy drinking with you.

The Hotel-Restaurant Management, Beverage Management, and Hospitality Management faculty at Sullivan University's National Center for Hospitality Studies: Anne Sandhu, Dawn McGiffen, and D. Stuart Wilson. I enjoy working with an "A-team" every day.

John Peter Laloganes, my friend. I appreciate your advice and support.

Bill Noel, my friend and mentor. Thank you for your ideas and support and, most of all, for sharing your experience.

Adam Segar, my friend. I am grateful for your advice and energy; you constantly raise the bar.

Scot Duval, who provided counsel and friendship.

Laura Sutton, who supported this project from the beginning, when I first pitched the idea.

Ashley Runyon, who picked up this book and ran with it across the goal line.

Joy Perrine, bartender extraordinaire. Thank you for your business savvy and your energy.

Chancellor A. R. Sullivan, who leads the university where I work. Thank you for your support.

President Glenn Sullivan, who shared his love of the Bluegrass State's beverage, bourbon, and provided good advice and support.

Dr. Eric Harter, who believed in me.

Dr. Jay Marr, who offered support and advice.

Dr. Stephen Coppock, my friend and mentor. Thank you for always seeing the light side of everything and for our jokes.

Keith Lerme, dean of the National Center for Hospitality Studies. Thank you for your leadership and sense of humor.

David H. Dodd, MBE. Thank you for leading by example and for your perspective and wisdom.

Allen Akmon, John Foster, Kimberly Jones, Derek Spendlove, Pam Hamilton, and Rob Beighey, the chairs of the programs at Sullivan University's National Center for Hospitality Studies. Thank you for your leadership and example.

Finally, I would like to thank the following artists, whose music I listened to while writing this book: Keb Mo, Albert Cummings, B. B. King, Buddy Guy, Darius Rucker, Dave Matthews, David Holmes, Dr. Dre, Elvis Presley, Eric Clapton, Etta James, Jay-Z, Jarrod Niemann, Johnny Cash, and Sheryl Crow.

Notes

1. THE OLD FASHIONED WHISKEY COCKTAIL

1. William Grimes, *Straight up or on the Rocks: The Story of the American Cocktail* (New York: North Point Press, 2001), 64.

2. David A. Embury, *The Fine Art of Mixing Drinks* (1948; reprint, New York: Mud Puddle Books, 2009), 125.

3. Olivier Said and James Mellgren, *The Bar: A Spirited Guide to Cocktail Alchemy* (Berkeley, Calif.: Ten Speed Press, 2005), 50.

4. Ti Adelaide Martin and Lally Brennan, *In the Land of Cocktails: Recipes and Adventures from the Cocktail Chicks* (New York: HarperCollins, 2007), 36.

5. Paul Harrington and Laura Moorehead, *Cocktail: The Drinks Bible for the 21st-Century* (New York: Viking, 1998), 134.

6. Embury, *The Fine Art of Mixing Drinks*, 123.

7. Kingsley Amis, *Everyday Drinking* (New York: Bloomsbury, 2008), 23.

8. David Wondrich, *Esquire Drinks* (New York: Hearst Books, 2002), 51.

9. Dale Degroff, *The Craft of the Cocktail* (New York: Clarkson Potter, 2002), 157.

10. Bob Lipinski and Kathie Lipinski, *Professional Beverage Management* (New York: John Wiley and Sons, 1996), 437.

11. Harvard Student Agencies Inc., *The Official Harvard Student Agencies Bartending Course* (New York: St. Martin's, 1995), 54–55.

12. Wondrich, *Esquire Drinks*, 50.

13. Ted Haigh, *Vintage Spirits and Forgotten Cocktails: From the Alamagoozlum to the Zombie and Beyond* (Beverly, Mass.: Quarry Books, 2009), 296.

14. Brad Thomas Parsons, *Bitters: A Spirited History of a Classic Cure-all with Cocktails, Recipes & Formulas* (Berkeley, Calif.: Ten Speed Press, 2011), 107.

15. Harrington and Moorehead, *Cocktail: The Drinks Bible*, 2.

16. Thomas Jefferson to Jean Guillaume Hyde de Neuville, December 13, 1818, in *The Writings of Thomas Jefferson*, Memorial Edition, vol. 15, ed. Albert Ellery Bergh (Washington, D.C.: Jefferson Memorial Association, 1905), 177–78.

17. David Wondrich, *Imbibe!* (New York: Penguin Group, 2007), 197.

18. Lafcadio Hearn, *La Cuisine Creole* (New Orleans: F. F. Hansell and Bro., 1885), 248.

19. Ibid.

20. George J. Kappeler, *Modern American Drinks* (New York: Merriam Company, 1895).

21. Jerry Thomas, *The Bar-Tender's Guide: How to Mix All Kinds of Plain and Fancy Drinks* (New York: Dick and Fitzgerald, 1887), 19, 20.

22. Haigh, *Vintage Spirits and Forgotten Cocktails*, 296.

23. Amis, *Everyday Drinking*, 42.

24. Said and Mellgren, *The Bar*, 130.

25. Gary Regan, *The Bartender's Bible* (New York: Harper-Collins, 1991), 18, 20.

26. Parsons, *Bitters*, 90.

27. Said and Mellgren, *The Bar*, 130.

28. Embury, *The Fine Art of Mixing Drinks*, 123–24.

29. Parsons, *Bitters*, 107.

30. Ibid., 9.

31. Thomas, *Bar-Tender's Guide*, 104.

32. Parsons, *Bitters*.

33. Martin and Brennan, *In the Land of Cocktails*, 39.

34. Ibid.

35. www.esquire.com/drinks/gin-cocktail-drink-recipe.

36. www.webtender.com/db/drink/905.

37. Regan, *Bartender's Bible*, 219.

38. Robert Hess, *The Essential Bartender's Pocket Guide* (New York: Mud Puddle Books, 2009), 74.

39. Embury, *The Fine Art of Mixing Drinks*, 124.

40. Jack Bettridge, "Make Mine American: Five Classic Cocktails Show American Whiskey in a New Light," *Wine Spectator*, January 31–February 29, 2012, 76.

2. PLACES, PEOPLE, AND THINGS

1. Gary Regan, *The Bartender's Bible* (New York: Harper-Collins, 1991), 219.

2. Albert Stevens Crockett, *Old Waldorf Bar Days* (New York: Aventine Press, 1931), 153.

3. William Grimes, *Straight up or on the Rocks: The Story of the American Cocktail* (New York: North Point Press, 2001), vii.

4. Ginger [Wallace Irwin], *The Book of Spice* (Boston: John W. Luce, 1906), 33–34.

5. Kurt Reighley, *United States of Americana* (New York: HarperCollins, 2010), 54.

3. RECIPES

1. Kingsley Amis, *Everyday Drinking* (New York: Bloomsbury, 2008), 23.

2. Olivier Said and James Mellgren, *The Bar: A Spirited Guide to Cocktail Alchemy* (Berkeley, Calif.: Ten Speed Press, 2005), 50.

3. Sheree Bykofsky and Megan Buckley, *Sexy City Cocktails: Stylish Drinks & Cool Classics You Can Sip with Attitude* (Avon, Mass.: Adams Media, 2003), 41.

4. Amis, *Everyday Drinking*, 22.

5. Williams-Sonoma, *The Bar Guide* (San Francisco: Weldon Owen, 2006), 219.

6. Ibid., 182.

7. Alison Leach, ed., *The Savoy Food and Drink Book* (Topsfield, Mass.: Salem House Publishers, 1988), 215.

8. Amis, *Everyday Drinking*, 23.

9. Ibid.

10. Ti Adelaide Martin and Lally Brennan, *In the Land of Cocktails: Recipes and Adventures from the Cocktail Chicks* (New York: HarperCollins, 2007), 39.

11. David Renton, *David Renton's Dorchester Cocktail Book* (London: George Weidenfeld and Nicolson, 1988), 27.

12. Ibid., 15.

13. Lynne Tolly and Pat Mitchamore, *Jack Daniel's Cookbook: The Spirit of Tennessee* (Nashville: Rutledge Hill Press,

1988); Vince Staten, *Jack Daniel's Old Time Barbecue Cookbook* (Louisville, Ky.: Sulgrave Press, 1991).

14. Lafcadio Hearn, *La Cuisine Creole* (New Orleans: F. F. Hansell and Bro., 1885), 248.

15. Ibid., 247.

16. Ibid., 249.

17. Ibid., 248.

18. George J. Kappeler, *Modern American Drinks* (New York: Merriam Company, 1895), 43.

19. Ibid.

20. Thomas Bullock, *The Ideal Bartender* (St. Louis: Buxton and Skinner Printing and Stationary Co., c. 1917).

21. William Grimes, *Straight up or on the Rocks: The Story of the American Cocktail* (New York: North Point Press, 2001), 99.

22. David A. Embury, *The Fine Art of Mixing Drinks* (1948; reprint, New York: Mud Puddle Books, 2009), 125.

23. www.esquire.com/drinks/gin-cocktail-drink-recipe.

24. Albert Stevens Crockett, *Old Waldorf Bar Days* (New York: Aventine Press, 1931), 153.

25. Irvin S. Cobb, *Irvin S. Cobb's Own Recipe Book* (Frankfort, Ky.: Frankfort Distilleries, 1934), 41–42.

26. Marion Flexner, *Out of Kentucky Kitchens* (New York: Bramhall House, 1949).

27. Elizabeth Ross, *Kentucky Keepsakes* (Kuttawa, Ky.: McClanahan Publishing House, 1996), 25.

28. Colonel Michael Edward Masters, *Hospitality Kentucky Style: Kentucky Heritage Grand Tour Kentucky Fine Foods & Spirits*, 2nd ed. (Bardstown, Ky.: Equine Writer's Press, 2003), 238.

29. Gary Regan, *The Bartender's Bible* (New York: HarperCollins, 1991).

30. Robert Hess, *The Essential Bartender's Pocket Guide* (New York: Mud Puddle Books, 2009).

31. Paul Harrington and Laura Moorehead, *Cocktail: The Drinks Bible for the 21st-Century* (New York: Viking, 1998).

32. Brad Thomas Parsons, *Bitters: A Spirited History of a Classic Cure-all with Cocktails, Recipes & Formulas* (Berkeley, Calif.: Ten Speed Press, 2011), 107.

33. Allan Gage, *Classic Cocktails from around the World* (London: Octopus Publishing Group, 2004).

34. Editors of *Imbibe* Magazine, *The American Cocktail: 50 Recipes that Celebrate the Craft of Mixing Drinks from Coast to Coast* (San Francisco: Chronicle Books, 2011), 27.

35. Parsons, *Bitters*, 216.

36. Jason Kosmas and Dushan Zaric, *Speakeasy* (Berkeley, Calif.: Ten Speed Press, 2010).

37. Jonathan Lundy, *Jonathan's Bluegrass Table: Redefining Kentucky Cuisine* (Louisville, Ky.: Butler Books, 2009).

38. Ibid., 137.

39. Said and Mellgren, *The Bar*, 173.

40. Scott Beattie, *Artisanal Cocktails* (Berkeley, Calif.: Ten Speed Press, 2008), 70.

41. Daniel Boulud and Xavier Herit, *Cocktails and Amuse-Bouches: For Him* (New York: Assouline Publishing, 2011), 40.

Bibliography

Abou-Ganim, Tony, with Mary Elizabeth Faulkner. *The Modern Mixologist*. Chicago: Surrey Books, 2010.

Amis, Kingsley. *Everyday Drinking*. New York: Bloomsbury, 2008.

Beattie, Scott. *Artisanal Cocktails*. Berkeley, Calif.: Ten Speed Press, 2008.

Bergh, Albert Ellery, ed. *The Writings of Thomas Jefferson*. Memorial Edition. Washington, D.C.: Jefferson Memorial Association, 1905.

Bettridge, Jack. "Make Mine American: Five Classic Cocktails Show American Whiskey in a New Light." *Wine Spectator*, January 31–February 29, 2012.

Boulud, Daniel, and Xavier Herit. *Cocktails and Amuse-Bouches: For Him*. New York: Assouline Publishing, 2011.

Bullock, Thomas. *The Ideal Bartender*. St. Louis: Buxton and Skinner Printing and Stationary Co., c. 1917.

Bykofsky, Sheree, and Megan Buckley. *Sexy City Cocktails: Stylish Drinks & Cool Classics You Can Sip with Attitude*. Avon, Mass.: Adams Media, 2003.

Cobb, Irvin S. *Irvin S. Cobb's Own Recipe Book*. Frankfort, Ky.: Frankfort Distilleries, 1934.

Connors, Thomas. *Meet Me in the Bar: Classic Drinks from America's Historic Hotels*. New York: Stewart, Tabori, Chang, 2003.

Crockett, Albert Stevens. *The Old Waldorf-Astoria Bar Book*. New York: A. S. Crockett, 1935.

———. *Old Waldorf Bar Days*. New York: Aventine Press, 1931.

Degroff, Dale. *The Craft of the Cocktail*. New York: Clarkson Potter, 2002.

———. *The Essential Cocktail: The Art of Mixing Perfect Drinks*. New York: Clarkson Potter, 2008.

Editors of *Imbibe* Magazine. *The American Cocktail: 50 Recipes that Celebrate the Craft of Mixing Drinks from Coast to Coast*. San Francisco: Chronicle Books, 2011.

Embury, David A. *The Fine Art of Mixing Drinks*. 1948. Reprint, New York: Mud Puddle Books, 2009.

Flexner, Marion. *Out of Kentucky Kitchens*. New York: Bramhall House, 1949.

Gage, Allan. *Classic Cocktails from around the World*. London: Octopus Publishing Group, 2004.

Giglio, Anthony. *Cocktails in New York: Where to Find 100 Classics and How to Mix Them at Home*. New York: Rizzoli, 2004.

Ginger [Wallace Irwin]. *The Book of Spice*. Boston: John W. Luce, 1906.

Grimes, William. *Straight up or on the Rocks: The Story of the American Cocktail*. New York: North Point Press, 2001.

Haigh, Ted. *Vintage Spirits and Forgotten Cocktails: From the Alamagoozlum to the Zombie and Beyond*. Beverly, Mass.: Quarry Books, 2009.

Harrington, Paul, and Laura Moorehead. *Cocktail: The Drinks Bible for the 21st-Century*. New York: Viking, 1998.

Harvard Student Agencies Inc. *The Official Harvard Student Agencies Bartending Course*. New York: St. Martin's, 1995.

Hearn, Lafcadio. *La Cuisine Creole*. New Orleans: F. F. Hansell and Bro., 1885.

Hess, Robert. *The Essential Bartender's Pocket Guide*. New York: Mud Puddle Books, 2009.

Jackson, Michael. *Whiskey: The Definitive World Guide*. London: DK Publishing, 2005.

Kappeler, George J. *Modern American Drinks*. New York: Merriam Company, 1895.

Kosmas, Jason, and Dushan Zaric. *Speakeasy*. Berkeley, Calif.: Ten Speed Press, 2010.

Leach, Alison, ed. *The Savoy Food and Drink Book*. Topsfield, Mass.: Salem House Publishers, 1988.

Lipinski, Bob, and Kathie Lipinski. *Professional Beverage Management*. New York: John Wiley and Sons, 1996.

Lubbers, Bernie. *Bourbon Whiskey: Our Native Spirit—Sour Mash and Sweet Adventures*. Indianapolis: Blue River Press, 2011.

Lundy, Jonathan. *Jonathan's Bluegrass Table: Redefining Kentucky Cuisine*. Louisville, Ky.: Butler Books, 2009.

Martin, Ti Adelaide, and Lally Brennan. *In the Land of Cocktails: Recipes and Adventures from the Cocktail Chicks*. New York: HarperCollins, 2007.

Masters, Colonel Michael Edward. *Hospitality Kentucky Style: Kentucky Heritage Grand Tour Kentucky Fine Foods & Spirits*, 2nd ed. Bardstown, Ky.: Equine Writer's Press, 2003.

Murphy, Brian D. *See, Mix, Drink: A Refreshingly Simple Guide to Crafting the World's Most Popular Cocktails*. New York: Little, Brown, 2011.

Pacult, F. Paul. *Kindred Spirits*. New York: Hyperion, 1997.

————. *Kindred Spirits 2*. New York: Spirits Journal, 2008.

Parsons, Brad Thomas. *Bitters: A Spirited History of a Classic Cure-all with Cocktails, Recipes & Formulas*. Berkeley, Calif.: Ten Speed Press, 2011.

Perrine, Joy, and Susan Reigler. *The Kentucky Bourbon Cocktail Book*. Lexington: University Press of Kentucky, 2009.

Reed, Ben. *Cool Cocktails: The Hottest New Drinks and the Best of the Classics*. New York: Ryland, Peters and Small, 2000.

Regan, Gary. *The Bartender's Bible*. New York: HarperCollins, 1991.

Regan, Gary, and Mardee Haidin Regan. *The Book of Bourbon and Other Fine American Whiskeys*. London: Mixellany Books, 2009.

Reighley, Kurt. *United States of Americana*. New York: HarperCollins, 2010.

Renton, David. *David Renton's Dorchester Cocktail Book*. London: George Weidenfeld and Nicolson, 1988.

Ross, Elizabeth. *Kentucky Keepsakes*. Kuttawa, Ky.: McClanahan Publishing House, 1996.

Said, Olivier, and James Mellgren. *The Bar: A Spirited Guide to Cocktail Alchemy*. Berkeley, Calif.: Ten Speed Press, 2005.

Sismondo, Christine. *America Walks into a Bar: A Spirited History of Taverns and Saloons, Speakeasies and Grog Shops*. New York: Oxford University Press, 2011.

Standage, Tom. *A History of the World in 6 Glasses*. New York: Walker, 2005.

Staten, Vince. *Jack Daniel's Old Time Barbecue Cookbook*. Louisville, Ky.: Sulgrave Press, 1991.

Thomas, Jerry. *The Bar-Tender's Guide: How to Mix All Kinds of Plain and Fancy Drinks*. New York: Dick and Fitzgerald, 1887.

Tolly, Lynne, and Pat Mitchamore. *Jack Daniel's Cookbook: The Spirit of Tennessee*. Nashville: Rutledge Hill Press, 1988.

Williams-Sonoma. *The Bar Guide*. San Francisco: Weldon Owen, 2006.

Wondrich, David. *Esquire Drinks*. New York: Hearst Books, 2002.

———. *Imbibe!* New York: Penguin Group, 2007.

Index

Recipe titles appear in **bold** *type.*